20 best
gluten-free
dessert recipes

Houghton Mifflin Harcourt
Boston • New York • 2013

For information about permission to reproduce selections from this book, write to Permissions, Houghton Mifflin Harcourt Publishing Company, 215 Park Avenue South, New York, New York 10003.

www.hmhco.com

Cover photo: Marble Cake (page 9)

General Mills
Food Content and Relationship Marketing Director: Geoff Johnson
Food Content Marketing Manager: Susan Klobuchar
Senior Editor: Grace Wells
Kitchen Manager: Ann Stuart
Recipe Development and Testing: Betty Crocker Kitchens
Photography: General Mills Photography Studios and Image Library

Houghton Mifflin Harcourt
Publisher: Natalie Chapman
Editorial Director: Cindy Kitchel
Executive Editor: Anne Ficklen
Associate Editor: Heather Dabah
Managing Editor: Rebecca Springer
Production Editor: Kristi Hart
Cover Design: Chrissy Kurpeski
Book Design: Tai Blanche

ISBN 978-0-544-31481-8
Printed in the United States of America

The Betty Crocker Kitchens seal guarantees
success in your kitchen. Every recipe has been
tested in America's Most Trusted Kitchens™
to meet our high standards of reliability, easy
preparation and great taste.

FIND MORE GREAT IDEAS AT
Betty Crocker.com

Dear Friends,

This new collection of colorful mini books has been put together with you in mind because we know that you love great recipes and enjoy cooking and baking but have a busy lifestyle. So every little book in the series contains just 20 recipes for you to treasure and enjoy. Plus, each book is a single subject designed in a bite-size format just for you—it's easy to use and is filled with favorite recipes from the Betty Crocker Kitchens!

All of the books are conveniently divided into short chapters so you can quickly find what you're looking for, and the beautiful photos throughout are sure to entice you into making the delicious recipes. In the series, you'll discover a fabulous array of recipes to spark your interest—from cookies, cupcakes and birthday cakes to party ideas for a variety of occasions. There's grilled foods, potluck favorites and even gluten-free recipes too.

You'll love the variety in these mini books—so pick one or choose them all for your cooking pleasure.

Enjoy and happy cooking!

Sincerely,

Betty Crocker

contents

Delicious Cakes

Mini Cakes

Scrumptious Pies

Chocolate-Orange Cake with Ganache Glaze

Prep Time: 40 Minutes • **Start to Finish:** 2 Hours 30 Minutes • Makes 10 servings

Cake

1 box Betty Crocker® Gluten Free devil's food cake mix

1 cup water

½ cup butter, softened

3 whole eggs

Filling

½ cup sugar

2 tablespoons cornstarch

½ cup orange juice

¼ cup water

2 egg yolks, lightly beaten

2 tablespoons butter

1½ teaspoons grated orange peel

Glaze

6 oz semisweet baking chocolate, finely chopped

½ cup whipping cream

4 teaspoons butter

1　Heat oven to 350°F (325°F for dark or nonstick pan). Generously spray bottom only of 8- or 9-inch round cake pan with cooking spray (without flour).

2　In large bowl, beat all cake ingredients with electric mixer on low speed 30 seconds, then on medium speed 2 minutes, scraping bowl occasionally. Pour into pan.

3　Bake 43 to 48 minutes or until toothpick inserted in center comes out clean. Cool 10 minutes. Run knife around edge of pan to loosen cake; remove from pan to cooling rack. Cool completely, about 1 hour.

4　Meanwhile, in 1-quart saucepan, mix sugar and cornstarch. Gradually stir in orange juice, ¼ cup water and the egg yolks. Cook over medium heat, stirring constantly, until thickened. Cook and stir 1 minute longer. Remove from heat; stir in 2 tablespoons butter and the orange peel. Transfer filling to small bowl. Cover; refrigerate 30 minutes.

5　In medium bowl, place chocolate. In 1-quart saucepan, heat whipping cream and 4 teaspoons butter over medium heat until butter melts and mixture boils. Pour cream mixture over chocolate; stir until smooth. Cool 10 minutes or until room temperature.

6　Cut cake horizontally to make 2 layers. On cut side of bottom layer, spread filling; cover with top layer. Pour glaze over top of cake; spread glaze to edge of cake and allow to drizzle down side of cake. Store in refrigerator.

1 Serving: Calories 490; Total Fat 25g (Saturated Fat 15g, Trans Fat 0.5g); Cholesterol 150mg; Sodium 360mg; Total Carbohydrate 60g (Dietary Fiber 2g); Protein 4g **Exchanges:** 1 Starch, 3 Other Carbohydrate, 5 Fat **Carbohydrate Choices:** 4

Tip　For a smooth filling, mix the sugar and cornstarch thoroughly before adding liquid. This keeps the cornstarch from developing lumps during cooking.

Chocolate Cake with Praline Topping

Prep Time: 20 Minutes • **Start to Finish:** 2 Hours • Makes 12 servings

Cake

1 box Betty Crocker Gluten Free devil's food cake mix

1 cup water

½ cup butter, softened

3 eggs

Topping

¼ cup butter or margarine

1 cup packed brown sugar

⅓ cup whipping cream

1 cup powdered sugar

1 teaspoon gluten-free vanilla

1 cup chopped pecans, toasted*

1 Heat oven to 350°F (325°F for dark or nonstick pan). Spray bottom only of 8- or 9-inch square pan with cooking spray (without flour).

2 In large bowl, beat all cake ingredients with electric mixer on low speed 30 seconds, then on medium speed 2 minutes, scraping bowl occasionally. Pour into pan.

3 Bake 8-inch pan 44 to 49 minutes, 9-inch pan 38 to 43 minutes, or until toothpick inserted in center comes out clean. Cool 10 minutes. Run knife around edge of pan to loosen cake; remove from pan to cooling rack. Cool completely, about 1 hour.

4 Meanwhile, in 2-quart saucepan, heat ¼ cup butter, the brown sugar and whipping cream to boiling, stirring frequently. Boil and stir 1 minute; remove from heat. Stir in powdered sugar and vanilla until smooth. Stir in pecans. Cool 10 to 15 minutes, stirring occasionally, until topping begins to thicken.

5 Spread warm topping over cake. Cool before serving. Cut into 4 rows by 3 rows.

To toast pecans, spread in ungreased shallow pan. Bake uncovered at 350°F 6 to 10 minutes, stirring occasionally, until light brown.

1 Serving: Calories 450; Total Fat 22g (Saturated Fat 10g, Trans Fat 0.5g); Cholesterol 90mg; Sodium 310mg; Total Carbohydrate 60g (Dietary Fiber 1g); Protein 3g **Exchanges:** 1 Starch, 3 Other Carbohydrate, 4 Fat **Carbohydrate Choices:** 4

Tip Use dark brown sugar for a robust praline flavor. Pralines are a patty-shaped Louisiana confection made from pecans, sugar and cream.

Pumpkin-Almond-Chocolate Torte

Prep Time: 25 Minutes • **Start to Finish:** 4 Hours 10 Minutes • Makes 20 servings

2 boxes Betty Crocker Gluten Free devil's food cake mix

Water, butter and eggs called for on cake mix box

1½ teaspoons gluten-free almond extract

2 cups whipping cream

½ cup powdered sugar

1 teaspoon pumpkin pie spice

2 teaspoons gluten-free vanilla

1 cup canned pumpkin (not pumpkin pie mix)

⅓ cup coarsely chopped gluten-free candied almonds

1 Heat oven to 350°F (325°F for dark or nonstick pans). Generously grease bottoms only of 2 (9-inch) round cake pans with shortening.

2 Make cake mix as directed on box, using water, butter and eggs and stirring in almond extract. Bake as directed. Cool 10 minutes; run knife around edge of pans to loosen cake. Remove cakes from pans to cooling racks. Cool completely, about 1 hour.

3 In chilled large bowl, beat whipping cream, powdered sugar, pumpkin pie spice and vanilla with electric mixer on high speed until stiff peaks form. Fold in pumpkin.

4 Cut each cake horizontally to make 2 layers. Place 1 bottom layer, cut side up, on serving plate; top with one-fourth of the whipped cream mixture. Top with another cake layer, cut side down. Top with one-fourth of whipped cream mixture. Repeat with remaining 2 layers and whipped cream mixture. Sprinkle with almonds. Refrigerate 2 hours. Cover and refrigerate any remaining torte.

1 Serving: Calories 310; Total Fat 15g (Saturated Fat 9g, Trans Fat 0g); Cholesterol 0mg; Sodium 300mg; Total Carbohydrate 43g (Dietary Fiber 1g); Protein 3g **Exchanges:** 1 Starch, 2 Other Carbohydrate, 3 Fat **Carbohydrate Choices:** 3

Marble Cake

Prep Time: 20 Minutes • **Start to Finish:** 2 Hours 20 Minutes • Makes 12 servings

Yellow Cake

1 box Betty Crocker Gluten Free yellow cake mix

½ cup butter, softened

⅔ cup water

2 teaspoons gluten-free vanilla

3 eggs

Devil's Food Cake

1 box Betty Crocker Gluten Free devil's food cake mix

½ cup butter, softened

1 cup water

3 eggs

Frosting

3 cups powdered sugar

⅓ cup butter, softened

2 teaspoons gluten-free vanilla

3 oz unsweetened baking chocolate, melted, cooled

3 to 4 tablespoons milk

1 Heat oven to 350°F. Grease bottoms only of 2 (8- or 9-inch) round cake pans with shortening or cooking spray.

2 In large bowl, beat all yellow cake ingredients with electric mixer on low speed 30 seconds, then on medium speed 2 minutes, scraping bowl occasionally. Set aside.

3 In another large bowl, beat all devil's food cake ingredients on low speed 30 seconds, then on medium speed 2 minutes, scraping bowl occasionally.

4 Spoon yellow and devil's food batters alternately into pans, dividing evenly. Cut through batters with table knife in zigzag pattern for marbled design.

5 Bake 40 to 45 minutes or until toothpick inserted in center comes out clean. Cool on cooling racks 15 minutes. Remove from pans. Cool completely, top side up, about 1 hour.

6 In medium bowl, beat powdered sugar and ⅓ cup butter with spoon or electric mixer on low speed until blended. Stir in 2 teaspoons vanilla and the chocolate. Gradually beat in just enough milk, 1 tablespoon at a time, to make frosting smooth and spreadable.

7 On serving plate, place 1 cake, rounded side down (trim rounded side if necessary so cake rests flat). Spread with ¼ cup frosting. Top with second cake, rounded side up. Frost side and top of cake with remaining frosting.

1 Serving: Calories 490; Total Fat 21g (Saturated Fat 12g, Trans Fat 0.5g); Cholesterol 120mg; Sodium 430mg; Total Carbohydrate 70g (Dietary Fiber 1g); Protein 4g **Exchanges:** 1½ Starch, 3 Other Carbohydrate, 4 Fat **Carbohydrate Choices:** 4½

Tip Butter is recommended for the success of this recipe.

Lemon-Filled Coconut Cake

Prep Time: 25 Minutes • **Start to Finish:** 2 Hours 25 Minutes • Makes 10 servings

Cake

1 box Betty Crocker Gluten Free yellow cake mix

½ cup butter, softened

⅔ cup water

2 teaspoons gluten-free vanilla

3 eggs

Frosting

2 cups powdered sugar

¼ cup butter, softened

1 teaspoon gluten-free coconut extract, if desired

1 to 2 tablespoons milk

Filling

½ cup lemon curd

1 cup flaked coconut, toasted*

1 Heat oven to 350°F (325°F for dark or nonstick pan). Spray bottom only of 8- or 9-inch round pan with cooking spray (without flour).

2 In large bowl, beat all cake ingredients with electric mixer on low speed 30 seconds, then on medium speed 2 minutes, scraping bowl occasionally. Pour batter into pan.

3 Bake 41 to 46 minutes or until toothpick inserted in center comes out clean. Cool 10 minutes. Run knife around side of pan to loosen cake; remove from pan to cooling rack. Cool completely, about 1 hour.

4 In medium bowl, beat powdered sugar and ¼ cup butter with electric mixer on low speed. Stir in coconut extract and 1 tablespoon milk. Gradually beat in just enough remaining milk, 1 teaspoon at a time, until frosting is smooth and spreadable.

5 Split cake horizontally to make 2 layers. On cut side of bottom layer, spread lemon curd; top with ½ cup of the coconut. Cover with top layer. Frost top and side of cake with frosting. Sprinkle coconut over top of cake. Refrigerate loosely covered.

1 Serving: Calories 500; Total Fat 21g (Saturated Fat 14g, Trans Fat 0.5g); Cholesterol 110mg; Sodium 360mg; Total Carbohydrate 72g (Dietary Fiber 1g); Protein 3g **Exchanges:** 1½ Starch, 3½ Other Carbohydrate, 4 Fat **Carbohydrate Choices:** 5

Tip Look for lemon curd in the jams and preserves aisle of the grocery store. Most stores stock lemon-flavored curd, but try orange or raspberry curd if it's available.

Berries 'n Cream Cake

Prep Time: 20 Minutes • **Start to Finish:** 1 Hour 15 Minutes • Makes 9 servings

Cake

1 box Betty Crocker Gluten
Free yellow cake mix

⅛ teaspoon ground nutmeg

½ cup cold butter or
margarine

⅔ cup milk

2 teaspoons gluten-free
vanilla

2 eggs

Berries

6 cups mixed fresh berries
(blueberries, raspberries,
sliced strawberries)

½ cup granulated sugar

Sweetened Whipped Cream

1½ cups whipping cream

3 tablespoons powdered
sugar

1 Heat oven to 375°F (350°F for dark or nonstick pan). Spray bottom only of 8- or 9-inch square pan with cooking spray (without flour).

2 In large bowl, stir cake mix and nutmeg. Cut in butter, using pastry blender or fork, until crumbly. In small bowl, with whisk, beat milk, vanilla and eggs; stir into cake mix mixture until moistened. Spread in pan.

3 Bake 30 to 35 minutes or until toothpick inserted in center comes out clean.

4 Meanwhile, in another large bowl, stir berries and granulated sugar until mixed; set aside to allow juice to form.

5 Cool cake 10 minutes. Run knife around edge of pan to loosen cake. Cool at least 10 minutes longer. In chilled large bowl, beat whipping cream and powdered sugar with electric mixer on low speed until mixture begins to thicken. Gradually increase speed to high, beating just until soft peaks form.

6 Cut into 3 rows by 3 rows. Cut each piece horizontally in half. Spoon half of the berries and sweetened whipped cream over bottom cake pieces; cover with top cake pieces. Spoon remaining berries and whipped cream over cake.

1 Serving: Calories 510; Total Fat 24g (Saturated Fat 15g, Trans Fat 1g); Cholesterol 120mg; Sodium 360mg; Total Carbohydrate 68g (Dietary Fiber 3g); Protein 5g **Exchanges:** 2 Starch, ½ Fruit, 2 Other Carbohydrate, 4½ Fat **Carbohydrate Choices:** 4½

Tip Substitute sliced fresh peaches for the berries. First, squeeze a bit of lemon juice over the peaches to keep them from browning.

Sticky Pecan-Caramel Fig Cakes

Prep Time: 20 Minutes • **Start to Finish:** 45 Minutes • Makes 24 cakes

1 cup packed brown sugar

1 cup chopped pecans

½ teaspoon salt

1 cup butter, softened

1 box Betty Crocker Gluten Free yellow cake mix

1 teaspoon ground cinnamon

1 teaspoon ground nutmeg

⅔ cup water

3 eggs

1 cup fig preserves

1 Heat oven to 350°F. Grease 24 regular-size muffin cups with shortening.

2 In large bowl, place brown sugar, pecans and salt. Using pastry blender or fork, cut in ½ cup of the butter until mixture is crumbly. Spoon about 1 tablespoon of the brown sugar mixture in bottom of each muffin cup; press gently to flatten.

3 In large bowl, beat cake mix, cinnamon, nutmeg, the remaining ½ cup butter, water and eggs with electric mixer on low speed 30 seconds, then on medium speed 2 minutes, scraping bowl occasionally. Add preserves; beat 30 seconds. Spoon about ¼ cup cake batter over crumbly mixture in each muffin cup.

4 Bake 20 to 25 minutes or until cake is golden brown. Remove from oven; immediately place cooling rack over top of pan. Turn upside down to release cakes. Serve warm.

1 Cake: Calories 250; Total Fat 12g (Saturated Fat 5g, Trans Fat 0g); Cholesterol 45mg; Sodium 210mg; Total Carbohydrate 34g (Dietary Fiber 0g); Protein 1g **Exchanges:** ½ Starch, 2 Other Carbohydrate, 2 Fat **Carbohydrate Choices:** 2

Vanilla Cupcakes with Caramel–Sea Salt Frosting

Prep Time: 25 Minutes • **Start to Finish:** 1 Hour 55 Minutes • Makes 12 cupcakes

Cupcakes

1 box Betty Crocker Gluten Free yellow cake mix

½ cup butter, softened

⅔ cup water

2 teaspoons gluten-free vanilla

3 eggs

Frosting

¼ cup butter

⅔ cup packed brown sugar

2 tablespoons milk

½ teaspoon gluten-free vanilla

1 cup powdered sugar

¼ teaspoon coarse sea salt

1 Heat oven to 350°F (325°F for dark or nonstick pan). Place paper baking cup in each of 12 regular-size muffin cups.

2 In large bowl, beat all cupcake ingredients with electric mixer on low speed 30 seconds, then on medium speed 2 minutes, scraping bowl occasionally. Divide batter evenly among muffin cups.

3 Bake 18 to 23 minutes or until toothpick inserted in center comes out clean. Cool 5 minutes; remove from pan to cooling rack. Cool completely, about 1 hour.

4 Meanwhile, in 2-quart heavy saucepan, melt ¼ cup butter over medium heat. Stir in brown sugar with whisk. Heat to boiling, stirring constantly. Stir in milk. Return to boiling. Remove from heat; cool until lukewarm, about 30 minutes. Stir in ½ teaspoon vanilla; gradually stir in powdered sugar until spreadable (add additional milk, 1 teaspoon at a time, if frosting becomes too thick). Frost cupcakes. Sprinkle with sea salt.

1 Cupcake: Calories 340; Total Fat 13g (Saturated Fat 8g, Trans Fat 0g); Cholesterol 85mg; Sodium 340mg; Total Carbohydrate 53g (Dietary Fiber 0g); Protein 2g **Exchanges:** 1 Starch, 2½ Other Carbohydrate, 2½ Fat **Carbohydrate Choices:** 3½

Tip Sprinkle salt on cupcakes immediately after frosting each one so salt adheres to the frosting before it stiffens.

Apple-Spice Cupcakes with Maple–Cream Cheese Frosting

Prep Time: 40 Minutes • **Start to Finish:** 1 Hour 40 Minutes • Makes 16 cupcakes

1 box Betty Crocker Gluten Free yellow cake mix

1 teaspoon ground cinnamon

½ teaspoon ground nutmeg

⅔ cup water

½ cup butter, softened

2 teaspoons gluten-free vanilla

3 eggs

1 cup chopped peeled apple

½ cup unsalted butter, softened

6 oz gluten-free cream cheese, softened

3½ tablespoons pure maple syrup

2 cups powdered sugar

¼ cup gluten-free glazed walnuts, chopped

1 Heat oven to 350°F. Place paper baking cup in each of 16 regular-size muffin cups. In large bowl, beat cake mix, cinnamon, nutmeg, water, ½ cup butter, the vanilla and eggs with electric mixer on low speed 30 seconds, then on medium speed 2 minutes, scraping bowl occasionally. Stir in apple. Divide batter evenly among muffin cups.

2 Bake 18 to 23 minutes or until toothpick inserted in center comes out clean. Cool 5 minutes; remove from pan to cooling rack. Cool completely, about 30 minutes.

3 In large bowl, beat ½ cup unsalted butter, cream cheese and maple syrup with electric mixer on medium speed until fluffy. Add powdered sugar; beat until smooth. Pipe or spread frosting onto cooled cupcakes. Sprinkle with glazed walnuts. Store loosely covered in refrigerator.

1 Cupcake: Calories 340; Total Fat 17g (Saturated Fat 10g, Trans Fat 0.5g); Cholesterol 80mg; Sodium 230mg; Total Carbohydrate 43g (Dietary Fiber 0g); Protein 2g **Exchanges:** 1 Starch, 2 Other Carbohydrate, 3 Fat **Carbohydrate Choices:** 3

Banana Cupcakes with Browned Butter Frosting

Prep Time: 20 Minutes • **Start to Finish:** 1 Hour 15 Minutes • Makes 17 cupcakes

Cupcakes

1 box Betty Crocker Gluten Free yellow cake mix

1 cup mashed ripe bananas (2 medium)

⅓ cup butter, melted*

⅓ cup water

3 eggs, beaten

2 teaspoons gluten-free vanilla

Frosting

⅓ cup butter*

3 cups gluten-free powdered sugar

1 teaspoon gluten-free vanilla

3 to 4 tablespoons milk

1 Heat oven to 350°F. Place paper baking cup in each of 17 regular-size muffin cups. In a large bowl, stir all cupcake ingredients until ingredients are moist. Divide batter evenly among muffin cups.

2 Bake 16 to 18 minutes or until golden brown. Remove from pan to cooling rack. Cool completely, about 30 minutes.

3 In small saucepan, heat ⅓ cup butter over medium heat just until light brown, stirring occasionally. Remove from heat. Cool slightly, about 5 minutes.

4 In medium bowl, beat butter, powdered sugar, vanilla and enough milk until smooth and spreadable. Frost cupcakes.

Do not use margarine or vegetable oil spreads.

1 Cupcake: Calories 270; Total Fat 8g (Saturated Fat 5g, Trans Fat 0g); Cholesterol 55mg; Sodium 200mg; Total Carbohydrate 46g (Dietary Fiber 0g); Protein 2g **Exchanges:** ½ Starch, 2½ Other Carbohydrate, 1½ Fat **Carbohydrate Choices:** 3

Tip *Beurre noisette* is the French term for "browned butter," referring to butter that becomes light hazelnut in color during cooking. The wonderful, unforgettable, one-of-kind flavor has no equal or substitution.

Tiramisu Cupcakes

Prep Time: 45 Minutes • **Start to Finish:** 1 Hour 40 Minutes • Makes 24 cupcakes

Cupcakes

2 boxes Betty Crocker Gluten
Free yellow cake mix

2 cups butter, softened

1⅓ cups water

4 teaspoons gluten-free
vanilla

6 eggs

Frosting

2 cups whipping cream

1 container (8 oz) gluten-free
mascarpone cheese

3 tablespoons coffee-flavored
liqueur

1 tablespoon cold brewed
coffee

1 cup powdered sugar

¼ cup coffee-flavored liqueur

⅛ teaspoon unsweetened
baking cocoa

¼ cup dark chocolate
shavings

1 Heat oven to 350°F. Place paper baking cup in each of 24 regular-size muffin cups. In large bowl, beat cake mixes, butter, water, vanilla and eggs with electric mixer on low speed 30 seconds, then on medium speed 2 minutes, scraping bowl occasionally. Divide batter evenly among muffin cups.

2 Bake 20 to 25 minutes or until toothpick inserted in center comes out clean. Cool 5 minutes; remove from pan to cooling rack. Cool completely, about 30 minutes.

3 In large bowl, beat whipping cream with electric mixer on high speed until stiff. Add mascarpone cheese, 3 tablespoons liqueur, the cold brewed coffee and powdered sugar; beat just until well blended and thick enough to pipe or spread (do not overbeat).

4 In shallow bowl, place ¼ cup liqueur. Dip tops of each cooled cupcake into liqueur. Top with whipped cream mixture. Sprinkle with cocoa and chocolate shavings. Store loosely covered in refrigerator.

1 Cupcake: Calories 400; Total Fat 25g (Saturated Fat 15g, Trans Fat 1g); Cholesterol 120mg; Sodium 330mg; Total Carbohydrate 40g (Dietary Fiber 0g); Protein 3g **Exchanges:** 1 Starch, 1½ Other Carbohydrate, 5 Fat **Carbohydrate Choices:** 2½

Tip For a special touch, pipe some of the frosting mixture into the center of each cupcake using a pastry bag and tip before dipping in liqueur and topping with frosting.

Caleb's Peppermint Brownie Cakes

Prep Time: 20 Minutes • **Start to Finish:** 1 Hour 45 Minutes • Makes 12 cakes

1 box Betty Crocker Gluten Free brownie mix

¼ cup butter, melted

3 eggs

12 miniature chocolate-covered peppermint patties, unwrapped

¾ cup semisweet chocolate chips

3 gluten-free candy canes (2 inch), unwrapped, coarsely crushed

1 Heat oven to 350°F. Place paper baking cup in each of 12 regular-size muffin cups. In medium bowl, stir brownie mix, melted butter and eggs until well blended. Divide batter evenly among muffin cups. Place 1 peppermint patty on top of batter in each cup; press each patty into batter about ¼ inch.

2 Bake 18 to 22 minutes or until edges are firm. Cool 5 minutes; remove from pan onto cooling rack. Cool completely, about 1 hour.

3 In small microwavable bowl, microwave chocolate chips uncovered on High about 1 minute or until softened; stir until smooth. Drizzle melted chocolate over top of each brownie cake. Sprinkle with crushed candy canes.

1 Cake: Calories 330; Total Fat 12g (Saturated Fat 7g, Trans Fat 0g); Cholesterol 65mg; Sodium 130mg; Total Carbohydrate 51g (Dietary Fiber 2g); Protein 3g **Exchanges:** 1 Starch, 2½ Other Carbohydrate, 2 Fat **Carbohydrate Choices:** 3½

Tip For a festive touch, use red or green cupcake liners.

Chocolate Truffle Cakes

Prep Time: 40 Minutes • **Start to Finish:** 1 Hour 20 Minutes • Makes 46 truffle cakes

Cakes

1½ cups semisweet or bittersweet chocolate chips

¾ cup whipping cream

1 box Betty Crocker Gluten Free devil's food cake mix

Water, butter and eggs called for on cake mix box

Garnishes, if desired

Roasted cacao nibs

Chopped dark chocolate

Crystallized ginger

Dried sweetened cranberries

Chopped pistachio nuts

Shredded coconut, toasted*

Sliced almonds, toasted**

1 In medium glass bowl, place chocolate chips. In 2-cup glass liquid measuring cup, microwave whipping cream uncovered on High 1½ minutes, or until hot. Pour whipping cream over chocolate chips; let stand 5 minutes. Stir until smooth. Refrigerate about 40 minutes, stirring every 10 minutes, until thick.

2 Heat oven to 350°F. Spray 46 mini muffin cups with cooking spray.

3 Make cake batter as directed on box. Divide batter evenly among muffin cups, filling each with about 1½ measuring tablespoonfuls or until about three-fourths full.

4 Bake 11 to 14 minutes or until top springs back when lightly touched. Cool 5 minutes. Carefully remove from pan to cooling rack. Cool completely, about 20 minutes.

5 If necessary, heat chocolate mixture in microwave on Medium (50%) 20 seconds, stirring every 10 seconds until smooth and piping consistency. Place ½ cup chocolate mixture in decorating bag fitted with round tip with ⅛-inch opening. Insert tip into top center of 1 cake, about halfway down into cake. Gently squeeze decorating bag, pulling upward until cake swells slightly and filling comes to top. Repeat with remaining cakes.

6 Place remaining chocolate mixture in small microwavable bowl. Microwave uncovered on High about 30 seconds or just until soft enough to spoon over and glaze cakes. Stir until smooth. Spoon warm chocolate mixture over each cake. Top with garnishes, and store loosely covered in refrigerator.

*To toast coconut, spread in ungreased shallow pan. Bake uncovered at 350°F 5 to 7 minutes, stirring occasionally, until golden brown.

**To toast almonds, spread in ungreased shallow pan. Bake uncovered at 350°F 6 to 10 minutes, stirring occasionally, until light brown.

1 Truffle Cake: Calories 100; Total Fat 6g (Saturated Fat 3.5g, Trans Fat 0g); Cholesterol 25mg; Sodium 75mg; Total Carbohydrate 11g (Dietary Fiber 0g); Protein 1g **Exchanges:** ½ Starch, 1 Fat **Carbohydrate Choices:** 1

Tip   To make a festive serving tray or to present as gifts, place decorated truffle cakes in mini paper baking cups. Or, pack them in boxes and tie with ribbons.

Apple Pie

Prep Time: 50 Minutes • **Start to Finish:** 2 Hours 50 Minutes • Makes 8 servings

Crust

¾ cup potato starch flour

½ cup tapioca flour

½ cup white rice flour

¼ cup garbanzo and fava flour

¼ cup sweet white sorghum flour

1 tablespoon sugar

½ teaspoon salt

1 egg

¾ cup canola oil

¼ cup water

½ teaspoon cider vinegar

2 teaspoons xanthan gum

1 teaspoon guar gum

⅓ cup chopped walnuts

¼ cup sugar

Filling

5 cups chopped peeled apples (5 medium)

½ cup sugar

¼ cup water

⅛ teaspoon salt

1 teaspoon ground cinnamon

⅛ teaspoon ground nutmeg, if desired

2 tablespoons cornstarch

2 tablespoons water

1 Heat oven to 350°F. Spray bottom and sides of 9-inch glass pie plate with cooking spray (without flour). In medium bowl, mix all flours, 1 tablespoon sugar and ½ teaspoon salt; set aside.

2 In food processor, place egg, oil, ¼ cup water, the vinegar, xanthan gum and guar gum. Cover; process 2 minutes. Add flour mixture. Cover; process 1 minute or until well mixed. Place 1 cup of dough in medium bowl. Stir in walnuts and ¼ cup sugar; set aside. Press remaining dough (about 2 cups) in bottom and up side of pie plate.

3 In 3-quart saucepan, place apples, ½ cup sugar, ¼ cup water, ⅛ teaspoon salt, the cinnamon and nutmeg. Heat to boiling over high heat. Reduce heat to medium-low; cook 10 minutes, stirring occasionally.

4 In small bowl, mix cornstarch and 2 tablespoons water until smooth. Add to apple mixture; cook and stir about 1 minute or until thickened. Pour filling into crust. Crumble walnut dough evenly over filling.

5 Bake 55 to 60 minutes or until crust is medium brown and filling is bubbly. Cool at least 1 hour before serving.

1 Serving: Calories 510; Total Fat 25g (Saturated Fat 2g, Trans Fat 0g); Cholesterol 25mg; Sodium 200mg; Total Carbohydrate 68g (Dietary Fiber 3g); Protein 3g **Exchanges:** ½ Starch, 2 Fruit, 2 Other Carbohydrate, 5 Fat **Carbohydrate Choices:** 4½

Contributed by Jean Duane Alternative Cook www.alternativecook.com

Tip Most grocery stores feature a gluten-free section. If your store doesn't carry these flours, ask them to order them.

Crème de Menthe Brownie Pie

Prep Time: 30 Minutes • **Start to Finish:** 3 Hours • Makes 8 servings

Crust

1 box Betty Crocker Gluten Free brownie mix

¼ cup butter, melted

2 whole eggs

Filling

1 cup almond milk

1 teaspoon unflavored gelatin

⅓ cup sugar

2 egg yolks

2 tablespoons cornstarch

1 tablespoon crème de menthe

1 tablespoon white crème de cacao

⅛ teaspoon salt

4 oz (half of 8-oz container) frozen whipped topping, thawed

½ cup miniature semisweet chocolate chips

1 Heat oven to 350°F (325°F for dark or nonstick pan). Spray bottom only of 8- or 9-inch square pan with cooking spray (without flour).

2 In medium bowl, stir brownie mix, butter and eggs until well blended (batter will be thick). Spread in pan.

3 Bake 8-inch pan 28 to 31 minutes, 9-inch pan 26 to 30 minutes, or until toothpick inserted 2 inches from side of pan comes out almost clean. Cool completely in pan on cooling rack, about 1 hour.

4 Meanwhile, in 3-quart saucepan, mix all filling ingredients except whipped topping and chocolate chips. Cook over medium heat, stirring constantly with whisk until mixture starts to boil; boil and stir 1 minute longer until thickened. Remove from heat. Refrigerate in pan about 30 minutes or until cool.

5 Cut brownies into very small pieces, about 36. In 9-inch glass pie plate, press brownie pieces together on bottom and up side of plate. Stir whipped topping and chocolate chips into filling. Spoon into brownie crust and spread evenly. Refrigerate 1 hour before serving.

1 Serving: Calories 480; Total Fat 19g (Saturated Fat 11g, Trans Fat 0g); Cholesterol 120mg; Sodium 240mg; Total Carbohydrate 70g (Dietary Fiber 3g); Protein 5g **Exchanges:** 1½ Starch, 3½ Other Carbohydrate, 3½ Fat **Carbohydrate Choices:** 4½

Tip Reserve the other half of the container of whipped topping to add a dollop on each slice of pie. For a special touch, drizzle the pie with chocolate or hot fudge topping.

Blueberry Pie with Cornmeal Crust

Prep Time: 45 Minutes · **Start to Finish:** 4 Hours · Makes 8 servings

Crust

1 cup white rice flour

½ cup tapioca flour

¼ cup potato starch flour

½ cup cornmeal

2 tablespoons sugar

1 teaspoon xanthan gum

½ teaspoon salt

¼ teaspoon pumpkin pie spice

½ cup very cold unsalted butter, cut into ½-inch pieces

¼ cup very cold shortening, cut into ½-inch pieces

¼ cup ice water

Filling

5 cups fresh blueberries (about 1½ lb)

½ cup sugar

⅓ cup cornstarch

1 jar (12 oz) blueberry preserves

¼ cup unsalted butter, cut into small pieces

1 teaspoon grated lemon peel

1 tablespoon fresh lemon juice

⅛ teaspoon salt

1 egg, separated

1 tablespoon milk

1 tablespoon sugar

1 In food processor, place flours, the cornmeal, 2 tablespoons sugar, the xanthan gum, ½ teaspoon salt and the pumpkin pie spice. Cover; pulse, using quick on-and-off motions, until blended. Add ½ cup butter and the shortening. Cover; pulse until coarse crumbs form, about 5 seconds. Add water; pulse just until dough comes together. Divide dough in half; flatten each half into a disk. Wrap individually in plastic wrap; refrigerate until firm, about 15 minutes.

2 Meanwhile, in large bowl, toss blueberries, ½ cup sugar, ⅓ cup cornstarch, the preserves, ¼ cup butter, the lemon peel, lemon juice and ⅛ teaspoon salt; set aside.

3 Line cookie sheet with foil; place on lower oven rack to catch any drips. Heat oven to 375°F. Unwrap 1 dough disk (keep remaining dough refrigerated until ready to use). Between 2 sheets of cooking parchment paper generously sprinkled with rice flour, roll dough into 12-inch round about ¼ inch thick. Carefully peel off top piece of parchment paper; replace paper and turn round over. Peel off parchment paper from second side of dough and discard.

4 Carefully place upside-down 9-inch glass pie plate on dough round. Turn plate with dough over; carefully remove parchment paper and discard. Gently pat dough into plate, pressing together any cracks or tears. In small bowl, beat egg white. Brush over dough. Spoon filling into crust-lined plate.

5 Unwrap second dough disk. Between 2 sheets of cooking parchment paper generously sprinkled with rice flour, roll dough into 12-inch round about ¼ inch thick. Carefully peel off top piece of parchment paper; invert dough onto filling. Peel off parchment paper from second side of dough and discard. Using sharp knife, trim crusts even with edge of plate; crimp edge with fork to seal. Cut vents in top crust. In small bowl, beat egg yolk and milk. Brush over dough. Sprinkle with 1 tablespoon sugar.

6 Bake 1 hour to 1 hour 10 minutes or until crust is golden and filling is bubbly. Cool completely on cooling rack, about 2 hours.

1 Serving: Calories 640; Total Fat 25g (Saturated Fat 13g, Trans Fat 2g); Cholesterol 70mg; Sodium 210mg; Total Carbohydrate 100g (Dietary Fiber 4g); Protein 4g **Exchanges:** 2 Starch, ½ Fruit, 4 Other Carbohydrate, 5 Fat **Carbohydrate Choices:** 6½

Tip Want an all-butter crust? Go ahead and eliminate the shortening and add ¼ cup more butter.

Easy Strawberry Pie

Prep Time: 15 Minutes • **Start to Finish:** 3 Hours • Makes 8 servings

Crust

6 cups Rice Chex® cereal

⅓ cup sunflower or canola oil or ghee (measured melted)

3 tablespoons potato starch flour

¼ cup sugar

¼ teaspoon salt

1 egg

Filling

2 lb fresh strawberries, sliced (about 5 cups)

1 container (13.5 oz) glaze for strawberries

1 Heat oven to 350°F. Spray 10-inch glass pie plate with cooking spray (without flour).

2 In food processor, place cereal. Cover; process until crushed. Add remaining crust ingredients. Cover; process until incorporated. Press cereal mixture into pie plate, starting in center and pressing up side. Bake 15 minutes or until golden brown. Cool completely on cooling rack.

3 In large bowl, stir strawberries and glaze until covered. Spread filling in crust. Refrigerate 2 hours before serving.

1 Serving: Calories 250; Total Fat 10g (Saturated Fat 1g, Trans Fat 0g); Cholesterol 25mg; Sodium 280mg; Total Carbohydrate 37g (Dietary Fiber 2g); Protein 3g **Exchanges:** 1 Starch, 1½ Other Carbohydrate, 2 Fat **Carbohydrate Choices:** 2½

Contributed by Jean Duane Alternative Cook www.alternativecook.com

Tip Garnish slices with a dollop of whipped cream if desired. Soy whipped cream is available for those avoiding dairy products.

Cream Cheese–Pumpkin Pie

Prep Time: 25 Minutes • **Start to Finish:** 4 Hours 40 Minutes • Makes 8 servings

Crust

1 cup Bisquick® Gluten Free mix

5 tablespoons cold butter

3 tablespoons water

Filling

4 oz cream cheese, softened

2 tablespoons sugar

¼ teaspoon gluten-free vanilla

1 egg yolk

½ cup sugar

1 teaspoon ground cinnamon

¼ teaspoon ground ginger

¼ teaspoon ground nutmeg

Dash salt

1 cup canned (from 15-oz can) or smoothly mashed cooked pumpkin

½ cup evaporated milk

1 egg, slightly beaten

Whipped cream, if desired

1 Heat oven to 425°F. Grease 9-inch glass pie plate with shortening or cooking spray. In medium bowl, place Bisquick mix. Cut in butter with pastry blender or fork, until mixture looks like fine crumbs. Stir in water; shape into ball with hands. Press dough in bottom and up side of pie plate.

2 Bake 10 to 12 minutes or until lightly browned; remove from oven. Cool while preparing cream cheese and pumpkin fillings. Reduce oven temperature to 350°F.

3 In small bowl, beat cream cheese, 2 tablespoons sugar and the vanilla with electric mixer on low speed until well blended. Add egg yolk; beat well. Spread cream cheese mixture in bottom of partially baked pie crust.

4 In large bowl, mix ½ cup sugar, the cinnamon, ginger, nutmeg, salt, pumpkin, evaporated milk and egg. Carefully pour pumpkin mixture over cream cheese mixture. Bake at 350°F 15 minutes. Cover crust edge with strips of foil to prevent excessive browning; bake 30 to 40 minutes longer or until knife inserted in center comes out clean. Cool completely; about 1 hour 30 minutes. Refrigerate about 2 hours or until ready to serve. Garnish each serving with dollop of whipped cream. Cover and refrigerate any remaining pie.

1 Serving: Calories 270; Total Fat 14g (Saturated Fat 8g, Trans Fat 0g); Cholesterol 85mg; Sodium 280mg; Total Carbohydrate 33g (Dietary Fiber 1g); Protein 3g **Exchanges:** ½ Starch, 1½ Other Carbohydrate, 3 Fat **Carbohydrate Choices:** 2

Tip You can make this pie a day ahead of serving. Be sure to store in the refrigerator until you are ready to serve it.

Chocolate Chip Cookie Ice Cream Pie

Prep Time: 15 Minutes • **Start to Finish:** 2 Hours 30 Minutes • Makes 8 servings

1 box Betty Crocker Gluten Free chocolate chip cookie mix

½ cup butter, softened

1 teaspoon gluten free vanilla

1 egg, beaten

1 tablespoon unsweetened baking cocoa

1½ quarts gluten-free vanilla ice cream

½ cup gluten-free chocolate fudge topping

1 Heat oven to 350°F. In medium bowl, stir cookie mix, butter, vanilla and egg until soft dough forms. Divide dough in half (about 2 cups in each half). With half of the dough, shape, bake and cool cookies as directed on box. Reserve for another use.

2 Meanwhile, stir cocoa into remaining half of dough. Crumble dough onto cookie sheet with sides. Bake 8 to 10 minutes or until dough is baked through and just starting to turn light brown. Cool 5 minutes; toss with spatula to make crumbs.

3 In ungreased 9-inch glass pie plate, press 1 cup of the cookie crumbs. Place small scoops of ice cream in single layer over crust; sprinkle with ¾ cup of the crumbs. Top with remaining ice cream and crumbs. Cover; freeze at least 2 hours.

4 In small microwavable bowl, microwave chocolate fudge topping on High 10 to 15 seconds. Drizzle topping over pie just before serving.

1 Serving: Calories 670; Total Fat 30g (Saturated Fat 17g, Trans Fat 1g); Cholesterol 100mg; Sodium 550mg; Total Carbohydrate 93g (Dietary Fiber 1g); Protein 7g **Exchanges:** 2 Starch, 4 Other Carbohydrate, 6 Fat **Carbohydrate Choices:** 6

Tip Garnish each slice of pie with whipped topping and a maraschino cherry.

Apple Crisp

Prep Time: 15 Minutes • **Start to Finish:** 1 Hour • Makes 12 servings

Apples

6 large tart cooking apples, thinly sliced

1 teaspoon ground cinnamon

Topping

1 box Betty Crocker Gluten Free yellow cake mix

½ cup chopped nuts

½ cup butter, softened

1 teaspoon ground cinnamon

1 egg, beaten

Serve-With

Ice cream, if desired

1 Heat oven to 350°F. In large bowl, toss apples and 1 teaspoon cinnamon. Spread apples evenly in ungreased 13 x 9-inch pan.

2 In large bowl, mix cake mix and nuts. Using pastry blender or fork, cut in butter until crumbly. Add 1 teaspoon cinnamon and the egg; mix well. Sprinkle evenly over apples.

3 Bake about 45 minutes or until topping is light brown. Serve warm with ice cream.

1 Serving: Calories 300; Total Fat 11g (Saturated Fat 5g, Trans Fat 0g); Cholesterol 40mg; Sodium 250mg; Total Carbohydrate 46g (Dietary Fiber 2g); Protein 2g **Exchanges:** 1 Starch, ½ Fruit, 1½ Other Carbohydrate, 2 Fat **Carbohydrate Choices:** 3

Tip To help keep the crispy topping intact, use a wide spatula to remove the dessert from the pan.

Metric Conversion Guide

Volume

U.S. Units	Canadian Metric	Australian Metric
¼ teaspoon	1 mL	1 ml
½ teaspoon	2 mL	2 ml
1 teaspoon	5 mL	5 ml
1 tablespoon	15 mL	20 ml
¼ cup	50 mL	60 ml
⅓ cup	75 mL	80 ml
½ cup	125 mL	125 ml
⅔ cup	150 mL	170 ml
¾ cup	175 mL	190 ml
1 cup	250 mL	250 ml
1 quart	1 liter	1 liter
1½ quarts	1.5 liters	1.5 liters
2 quarts	2 liters	2 liters
2½ quarts	2.5 liters	2.5 liters
3 quarts	3 liters	3 liters
4 quarts	4 liters	4 liters

Weight

U.S. Units	Canadian Metric	Australian Metric
1 ounce	30 grams	30 grams
2 ounces	55 grams	60 grams
3 ounces	85 grams	90 grams
4 ounces (¼ pound)	115 grams	125 grams
8 ounces (½ pound)	225 grams	225 grams
16 ounces (1 pound)	455 grams	500 grams
1 pound	455 grams	0.5 kilogram

Note: The recipes in this cookbook have not been developed or tested using metric measures. When converting recipes to metric, some variations in quality may be noted.

Measurements

Inches	Centimeters
1	2.5
2	5.0
3	7.5
4	10.0
5	12.5
6	15.0
7	17.5
8	20.5
9	23.0
10	25.5
11	28.0
12	30.5
13	33.0

Temperatures

Fahrenheit	Celsius
32°	0°
212°	100°
250°	120°
275°	140°
300°	150°
325°	160°
350°	180°
375°	190°
400°	200°
425°	220°
450°	230°
475°	240°
500°	260°

Recipe Testing and Calculating Nutrition Information

Recipe Testing:

- Large eggs and 2% milk were used unless otherwise indicated.
- Fat-free, low-fat, low-sodium or lite products were not used unless indicated.
- No nonstick cookware and bakeware were used unless otherwise indicated. No dark-colored, black or insulated bakeware was used.
- When a pan is specified, a metal pan was used; a baking dish or pie plate means ovenproof glass was used.
- An electric hand mixer was used for mixing only when mixer speeds are specified.

Calculating Nutrition:

- The first ingredient was used wherever a choice is given, such as ⅓ cup sour cream or plain yogurt.
- The first amount was used wherever a range is given, such as 3- to 3½-pound whole chicken.
- The first serving number was used wherever a range is given, such as 4 to 6 servings.
- "If desired" ingredients were not included.
- Only the amount of a marinade or frying oil that is absorbed was included.

CPSIA information can be obtained
at www.ICGtesting.com
Printed in the USA
LVHW081947300522
720047LV00020B/469

9 780544 314818